Which Food Will You Choose?

Claire Potter • Ailie Busby

FEATHERSTONE

LONDON OXFORD NEW YORK NEW DELHI SYDNEY

Last Monday wasn't like normal Mondays. Mummy was in a bad mood! She couldn't find **anything** she wanted to make for dinner.

"Urggghhh!" she groaned.
"I'm so bored of **BEIGE!**
Beige chicken nuggets,
beige pasta, beige chips,
beige cereal, beige crisps...
What we need is some
COLOUR!"

"Come on," said Mummy. "Let's go!"

"Where?" we asked.

"To the **supermarket**," she said. "To play a game."

6

"But you can't play **games** in the supermarket," we said.
"Wait and see!" said Mummy.

7

"Right, are you ready?" said mummy.
"Choose **three** foods – anything
you like – but they have to be **RED**.
Bold, bright, beautiful **red**!"

"Okaaay!" we said.
We could already see
lots of red foods on
the shelves.

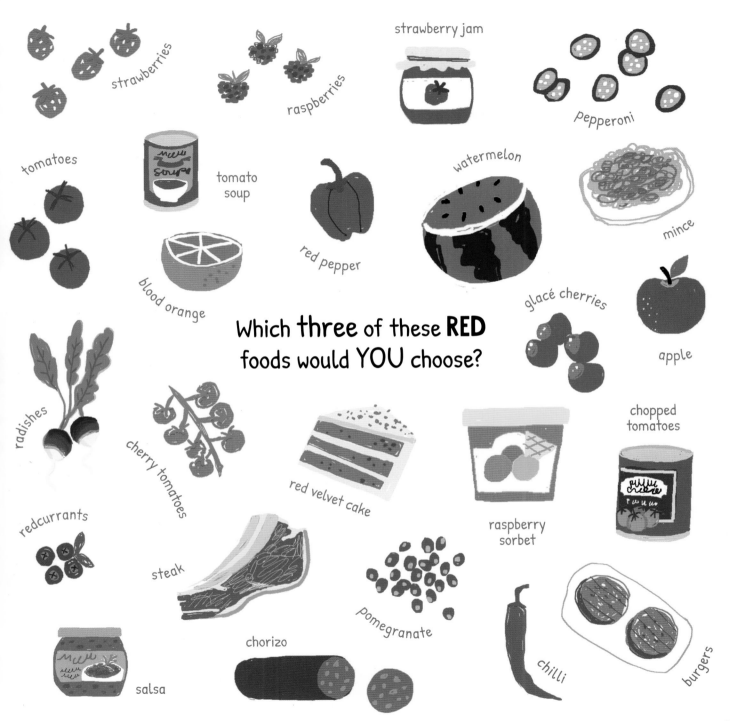

strawberries

raspberries

strawberry jam

pepperoni

tomatoes

tomato soup

watermelon

mince

red pepper

blood orange

glacé cherries

apple

Which **three** of these **RED** foods would YOU choose?

radishes

cherry tomatoes

red velvet cake

raspberry sorbet

chopped tomatoes

redcurrants

steak

pomegranate

salsa

chorizo

chilli

burgers

9

We chose **pepperoni**, **watermelon** and **tomato soup**.

When we got home, we made our own pizzas and decorated them with the **pepperoni**.

We ate the **watermelon** just as it was, but planted the seeds in pots to see if we could grow one.

And we took the **tomato soup** in a flask when we went to play in the park.

What would YOU do with the three RED foods you chose?

On **Tuesday**, we played the game again.
Mummy said, "Today, it's **YELLOW**. Strong,
sunshiney, smiley **yellow!** Ready. Steady. Go!"

There were **so many** yellow foods to choose from.

banana

piccalilli

holey cheese

lemon

Cheddar cheese

squash

mango

custard

yellow pepper

corn on the cob

egg noodles

lemon curd

Which three of these YELLOW foods would YOU choose?

quiche

honeydew melon

pilau rice

mustard

lemon drizzle cake

grapefruit

sweetcorn

pineapple

butter

crème caramel

macaroni cheese

egg mayonnaise

We chose **corn on the cob**, a **cheese with holes in it** and a **banana**.

When we got home, we ate the **corn on the cob** on sticks like lollies.

We spied on
Daddy through
the holey **cheese**

and then melted it on toast.

And we made a **banana**
split for pudding.

What would YOU do
with the **three YELLOW**
foods you chose?

On **Wednesday**, we went to the supermarket again. "This time, let's go for **GREEN**." said Mummy. "Gorgeous, glorious, groovy **green!**"

There were **gazillions** of green foods.

broccoli

pea soup

green pepper

cabbage

apple

avocado

olives

sugar snap peas

celery

pistachio nuts

cucumber

peas

gherkins

Which **three** of these **GREEN** foods would **YOU** choose?

seaweed

Brussels sprouts

leek

kiwi fruit

lime

coriander

mint choc chip ice cream

green pasta

cress

mushy peas

iceberg lettuce

We chose
celery,
olives and
green pasta.

When we got home, we dipped the **celery** in peanut butter and gave the ends to Bertie our rabbit.

We put the **olives** on
our fingers and ate
them one by one.

And we ate the **green pasta** with our eyes closed to see if it tasted
different to ordinary pasta.

What would
YOU do with the
three GREEN
foods you chose?

On **Thursday**, mummy said, "Okay, how about... **ORANGE?**
Zingy, zesty, zippety **orange!**"

We found **oodles** of orange foods.

red lentils

kippers

sweet potato

pumpkin

Red Leicester cheese

marmalade

lobster

butternut squash

nectarine

smoked salmon

carrot cake

dried apricots

orange pepper

Which **three** of these **ORANGE** foods would YOU choose?

crab

satsuma

sweet and sour sauce

peach

cantaloupe melon

dried papaya

carrots

ice lolly

baked beans

turmeric

carrot and coriander soup

We chose **satsumas**, **smoked salmon**
and a **carrot** that was a funny shape.

When we got home, we tried to peel the
skin off the **satsumas** in one piece.

We pretended the **smoked salmon** was our tongue before we ate it.

And we whizzed the **carrot** up into a smoothie.

What would YOU do with the **three ORANGE** foods that you chose?

On **Friday**, we asked "What colour today, Mummy?"
She said, "Today, I want you to choose three foods that are **PURP**..."

We were off before she could finish!

Look at **all** the purple foods we found.

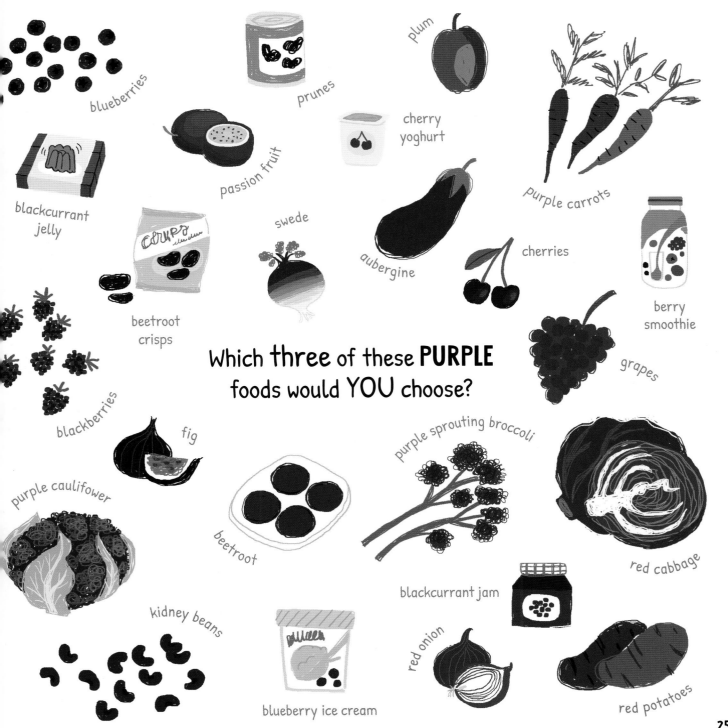

blueberries

prunes

plum

cherry
yoghurt

purple carrots

blackcurrant
jelly

passion fruit

swede

aubergine

cherries

berry
smoothie

beetroot
crisps

grapes

Which **three** of these **PURPLE**
foods would **YOU** choose?

blackberries

fig

purple sprouting broccoli

purple cauliflower

beetroot

red cabbage

blackcurrant jam

kidney beans

red onion

blueberry ice cream

red potatoes

25

We chose **blackcurrant jelly,** **beetroot** and **blueberries.**

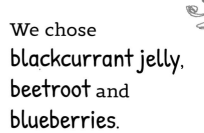

When we got home, we made the **blackcurrant jelly** in the shape of dinosaurs.

We had the **beetroot** in a salad. (Daddy said eating beetroot makes your wee-wee go pink!)

And we made the **blueberries** last all the way to Grandad's house by only eating one every time we spotted a cat or a dog.

What would YOU do with the **three PURPLE** foods that you chose?

The next day was **Saturday**. When we got up, we caught mummy having a croissant and coffee for breakfast.

"Urgggghhh!" we said,
"That's so **BEIGE!**"

So on **Sunday**, WE made breakfast for MUMMY.

HOW TO GET THE MOST OUT OF THIS BOOK

The aim of this book isn't to teach children that beige foods are bad. It's to encourage a curious, open-minded and adventurous attitude towards food. Enjoy the story with your child – and then play the game with them in the supermarket in real life!

WHEN READING THE BOOK TO YOUR CHILD

★ It's really important your child can relax and enjoy choosing ANY food from the page without feeling pressured to now eat that food in real life. So never judge their choices with comments like:

> But you never eat your peas when I give them to you!
>
> Shall I put cheese in your sandwiches tomorrow for a change then?
>
> You always choose ice cream – choose something healthy this time!

★ Do initiate 'neutral' conversation that encourages a curiosity about food:

> Kiwi fruit's all hairy, isn't it?
>
> I wonder why red cabbage is called red cabbage when it's purple!
>
> Do you remember when we saw crab at that market?

★ Avoid talking about which foods on the page they (or you!) LIKE and DON'T LIKE. This reinforces a rigid – rather than a flexible – mindset towards food.

★ Embrace whatever suggestions your child makes about how they would eat the foods – however silly or inappropriate they seem to you! Dip red pepper in jam? Eat blueberries in the bath? Make mushy peas into mountains?

WHEN PLAYING THE GAME IN REAL LIFE

★ The game is only fun and effective if your child feels they are genuinely in control of which three foods they choose. Don't make suggestions or judge their choices!

★ If you think your child is likely to head straight for sugary foods, tell them in advance that ONE of the foods can be sweet.

★ Ask them for ideas of how they'd like to eat the foods and involve them in the preparation. Children are more likely to eat something they feel 'ownership' of.

★ Don't put any pressure at all on your child to actually eat, or even try, the foods. This just gives them something to react AGAINST. Simple exposure to a food – seeing, smelling, touching, playing with it – is the first vital step towards becoming receptive to the idea of eating it.

★ Play the game once in a while to keep it fresh and fun – not every day for a week like the children in the story!

For a clear, simple, powerful approach to stop fussy eating, read Claire's book *Getting the Little Blighters to Eat* or visit her website stopfussyeating.uk

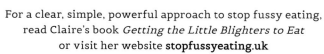